PIANO SOLO

2ND EDITION

Symphonic Classics

ISBN 0-7935-0060-5

HAL•LEONARD® CORPORATION
7777 W. BLUEMOUND RD. P.O. BOX 13819 MILWAUKEE, WI 53213

In Australia contact:
Hal Leonard Australia Pty. Ltd.
4 Lentara Court
Cheltenham, Victoria, 3192 Australia
Email: ausadmin@halleonard.com

T0050958

Visit Hal Leonard Online at
www.halleonard.com

Contents

Air on the G String
from Orchestral Suite No. 3 in D Major

Johann Sebastian Bach
1685–1750
BWV 1068
originally for orchestra

Largo
from Piano Concerto in F minor

Johann Sebastian Bach
1685-1750
originally for piano and orchestra

Piano Concerto No. 4 in G Major

First Movement Themes

Ludwig van Beethoven
1770-1827
originally for piano and orchestra

Symphony No. 5 in C minor
First Movement Theme

Ludwig van Beethoven
1770-1827
originally for orchestra

Allegro con brio

Symphony No. 9
Fourth Movement Excerpt

Ludwig van Beethoven
1770-1827
Op. 125
originally for chorus and orchestra

Allegro assai vivace

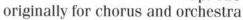

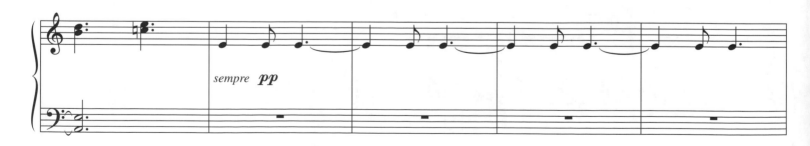

original key: D Major

Polovtsian Dance

from *Prince Igor*
First Theme

Alexander Borodin
1833-1887
originally for orchestra

original key: A Major

Symphony No. 1 in C minor

Fourth Movement Chorale

Johannes Brahms
1833-1897
originally for orchestra

Piano Concerto No. 2 in B flat Major
Second Movement Theme

Johannes Brahms
1833-1897
originally for piano and orchestra

Theme
from Variations on a Theme of Haydn

Johannes Brahms
1833-1897
originally for orchestra

Symphony No. 9 in E minor

"From the New World"
Second Movement Excerpt

Antonín Dvořák
1841-1904
Op. 95
originally for orchestra

Allegro Maestoso and Cantabile Themes

from Piano Concerto No. 1 in E minor

Fryderyk Chopin
1810-1849
originally for piano and orchestra

Trumpet Voluntary in D Major

Jeremiah Clarke
1673-1707
originally for trumpet and orchestra

35

Symphony in D minor
First Movement Themes

César Franck
1822-1890
originally for orchestra

THEME 1
Allegro non troppo

THEME 2

THEME 3

In the Hall of the Mountain King

from *Peer Gynt*

Edvard Grieg
1843–1907
originally for orchestra

Alla marcia e molto marcato

pp

sempre staccato e **pp**

Funeral March of a Marionette
Themes

Charles Gounod
1818-1893
originally for orchestra

Allegretto

47

Morning

from *Peer Gynt*

Edvard Grieg
1843-1907
originally for orchestra

Allegretto pastorale

Hornpipe
from *Water Music*

George Frideric Handel
1685-1759
originally for orchestra

Con brio

Air
from *Water Music*

George Frideric Handel
1685-1759
originally for orchestra

Andante con moto

Pastoral Symphony

from *Messiah*

George Frideric Handel
1685-1759
originally for orchestra

London Symphony
First Movement Excerpt

Franz Joseph Haydn
1732-1809
originally for orchestra

Les Préludes
Excerpted Melodies

Franz Liszt
1811-1886
originally for orchestra

The Swan
from *Carnival of the Animals*

Camille Saint-Saëns
1835-1921
originally for chamber ensemble

Piano Concerto No. 2 in D minor
Third Movement Themes

Felix Mendelssohn
1809-1847
originally for piano and orchestra

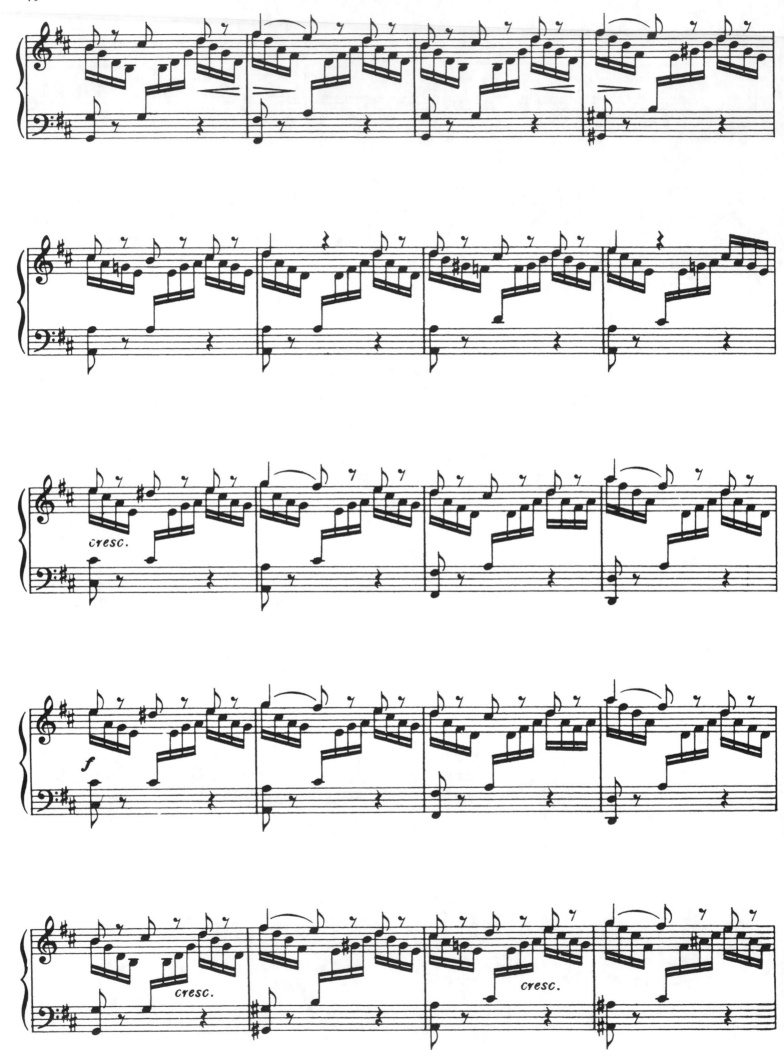

Piano Concerto No. 1 in G minor

Second Movement Theme

Felix Mendelssohn
1804-1847
originally for piano and orchestra

73

Rondeau

Excerpt

Jean-Joseph Mouret
1682-1738
originally for orchestra

Majestically

mp

75

Piano Concerto in A Major
First Movement Excerpt

Wolfgang Amadeus Mozart
1756-1791
K. 488
originally for piano and orchestra

Romance
from *Eine kleine Nachtmusik*

Wolfgang Amadeus Mozart
1756-1791
originally for small string ensemble

Romanza
from Piano Concerto in D minor

Wolfgang Amadeus Mozart
1756-1791
K. 466
originally for piano and orchestra

Symphony No. 40 in G minor

First Movement Excerpt

Wolfgang Amadeus Mozart
1756-1791
originally for orchestra

Can Can
from *Orpheus in the Underworld*

Jacques Offenbach
1819–1880
originally for orchestra

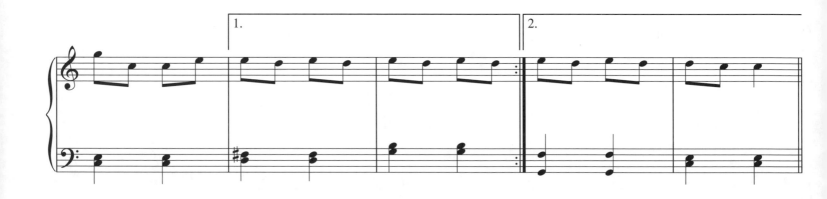

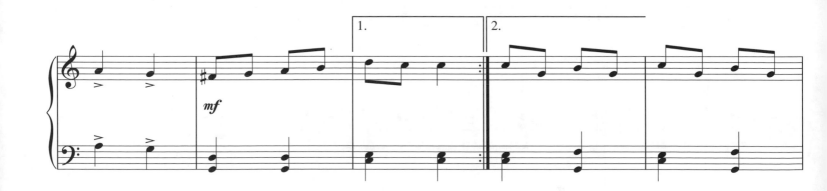

Canon
Excerpt

Johann Pachelbel
1653-1706
originally for 3 violins and continuo

original key: D Major

Scheherazade
Themes from Part 1

Nikolay Rimsky-Korsakov
1844-1908
Op. 35
originally for orchestra

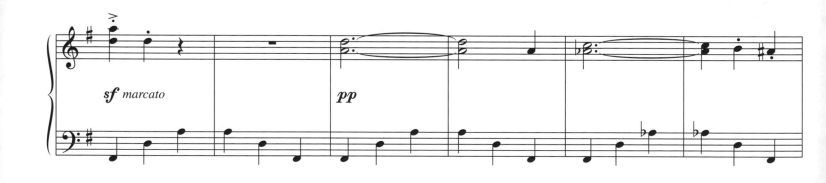

Andante
from Octet

Franz Schubert
1797-1828
Op. 166

Andante un poco mosso

Scherzo
from Symphony No. 1 in B flat Major

Robert Schumann
1810-1856
originally for orchestra

Andante Theme
from Symphony No. 4 in C minor "Tragic"

Franz Schubert
1797-1828
originally for orchestra

Piano Concerto in A minor
First Movement Excerpt

Robert Schumann
1810-1856
originally for piano and orchestra

Andante con moto
from Symphony No. 5 in E minor

Pyotr Il'yich Tchaikovsky
1840-1893
originally for orchestra

Andante cantabile, con alcuna licenza

Dance of the Sugar Plum Fairy

from *The Nutcracker*

Pyotr Il'yich Tchaikovsky
1840-1893
Op. 71
originally for orchestra

Andante ma non troppo

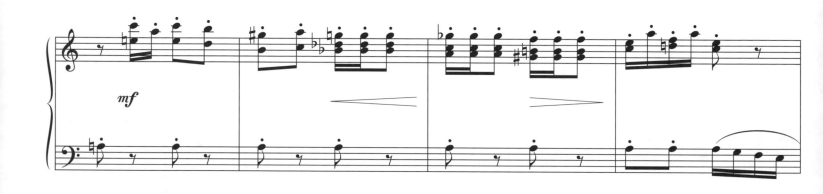

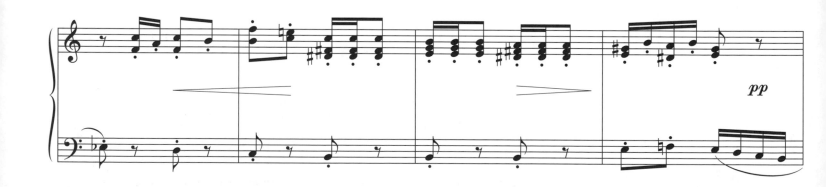

original key: E Minor

Piano Concerto No. 1 in B flat minor
Opening Theme

Pyotr Il'yich Tchaikovsky
1840-1893
originally for piano and orchestra

Love Theme
from *Romeo and Juliet*

Pyotr Il'yich Tchaikovsky
1840-1893
originally for orchestra

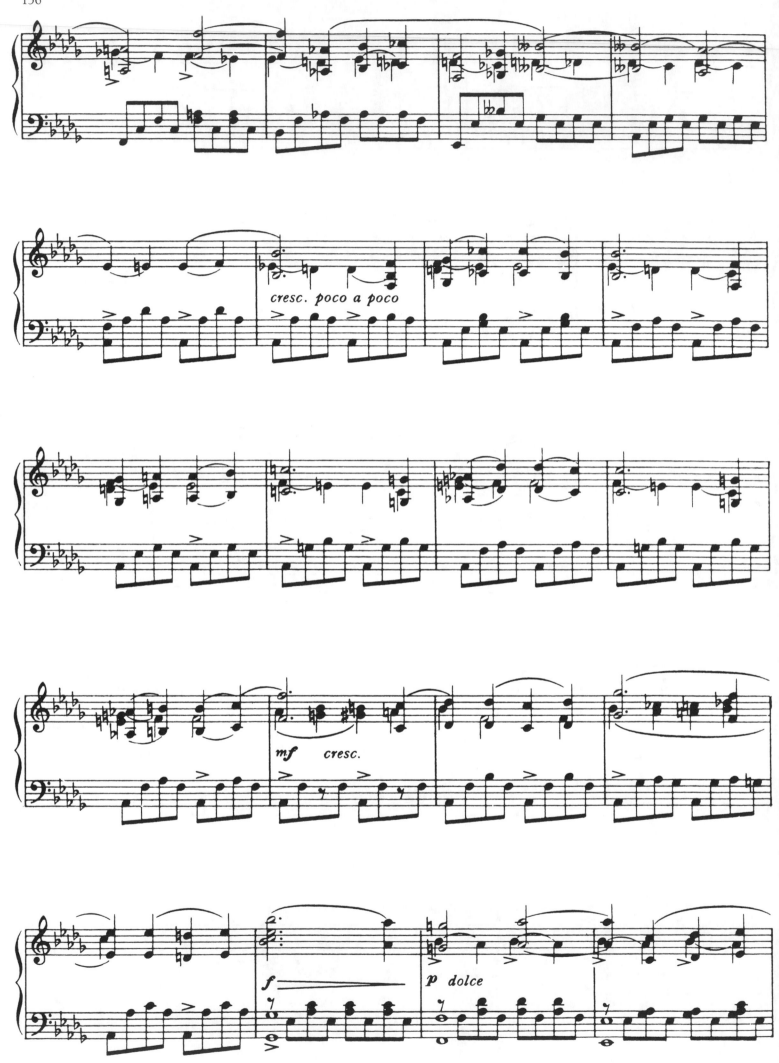

Piano Concerto No. 2 in G Major
Second Movement

Pyotr Il'yich Tchaikovsky
1840-1893
originally for piano and orchestra

140

Autumn

from *The Four Seasons*
First Movement Excerpt

Antonio Vivaldi
1678-1741
originally for violin and orchestra

THE WORLD'S GREAT CLASSICAL MUSIC

A beautiful library of hundreds of great classical compositions, conveniently published in sizable volumes, all with long-lasting sewn binding.

Visit our website at www.halleonard.com for a complete contents list for each volume!

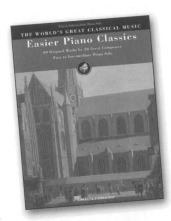

EASY TO INTERMEDIATE PIANO SOLO

THE BAROQUE ERA
00240057......................................$14.95

BEETHOVEN
00220034......................................$14.95

THE CLASSICAL ERA
00240061......................................$14.95

CLASSICAL MASTERPIECES
00290520......................................$14.95

EASIER PIANO CLASSICS
00290519......................................$14.95

FAVORITE CLASSICAL THEMES
00220021......................................$14.95

GREAT EASIER PIANO LITERATURE
00310304......................................$14.95

MOZART
00220028......................................$14.95

OPERA'S GREATEST MELODIES
00220023......................................$14.95

THE ROMANTIC ERA
00240068......................................$14.95

JOHANN STRAUSS
00220040......................................$14.95

THE SYMPHONY
00220041......................................$14.95

TCHAIKOVSKY
00220027......................................$14.95

FLUTE

THE BAROQUE AND CLASSICAL FLUTE
00841550   Flute and Piano $16.95

THE ROMANTIC FLUTE
00240210   Flute and Piano $12.95

PIANO/VOCAL

GILBERT & SULLIVAN
00740142......................................$16.95

INTERMEDIATE TO ADVANCED PIANO SOLO

BACH
00220037......................................$14.95

THE BAROQUE ERA
00240060......................................$14.95

BEETHOVEN
00220033......................................$14.95

THE CLASSICAL ERA
00240063......................................$14.95

GREAT CLASSICAL THEMES
00310300......................................$14.95

GREAT MASTERWORKS
00220020......................................$14.95

GREAT PIANO LITERATURE
00310302......................................$14. 95

MOZART
00220025......................................$14.95

OPERA AT THE PIANO
00310297......................................$14.95

PIANO CLASSICS
00290518......................................$14.95

PIANO PRELUDES
00240248......................................$16.95

THE ROMANTIC ERA
00240096......................................$14.95

JOHANN STRAUSS
00220035......................................$14.95

THE SYMPHONY
00220032......................................$14.95

TCHAIKOVSKY
00220026......................................$14.95

GUITAR

MASTERWORKS FOR GUITAR
00699503   Classical Guitar......................$16.95

CD-ROM SHEET MUSIC

110 CLASSICAL THEMES
00220030......................................$14.95

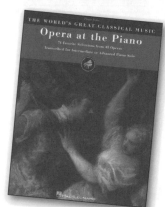

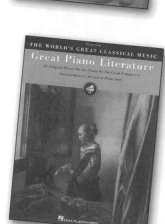

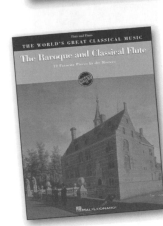

FOR MORE INFORMATION, SEE YOUR LOCAL MUSIC DEALER, OR WRITE TO:

HAL•LEONARD® CORPORATION
7777 W. BLUEMOUND RD. P.O. BOX 13819 MILWAUKEE, WI 53213

Visit Hal Leonard Online at **www.halleonard.com**   Prices, availability, and contents subject to change without notice.